MEENA ROHITH

FLIPPING ON THE LIGHTS

HEALING FROM SEXUAL ABUSE ACROSS ALL AGES.

FLIPPING

ON

THE LIGHTS.

Healing From Sexual Abuse Across All Ages.

Table of Contents

COPYRIGHT

Book cover and illustrations by Meena Rohith Vignesh.

DEDICATION

It's for the person sitting on their bathroom floor, unsure if they can make it through another day. It's for the friend who doesn't know what to say when someone confides in them. It's for the parent, partner, or sibling who wants to understand and support but feels lost.
To everyone who is disgusted about their own body but wants it to stop
For everyone who wants to take a stand for themselves
For everyone who needs to stop freezing and want to take action to gain their life back.

Sexual abuse is one of the darkest human experiences, but darkness doesn't stand a chance when we start flipping on the lights.

DESCRIPTION.

Flipping on the Lights is not merely a guide it is a book to make you move towards the healing path with worksheets references and even exercises to deeply understand the effect of abuse in day-to-day life, the mindset of the abusers so that you can forgive yourself emotionally, physically and spiritually. It talks about the benefits of breaking the silence and taking a stand for yourself.

This isn't some stiff, clinical textbook.

It's not here to overwhelm you with jargon or make you feel like you're sitting in a lecture hall. Think of it as a conversation over coffee (or wine—no judgment). A messy, heartfelt, and even sometimes funny (yes, funny) conversation about a topic that desperately needs light, love, and a whole lot of hope.

What this book *isn't*:

- A substitute for therapy (though it can be a great complement).
- A one-size-fits-all solution.
- A place for judgment or shame.

Why did I decide to write this?

When I remember my childhood abuse my family was still in contact with that Particular person I couldn't find the courage to tell my parents even when I did I was ignored, it affected every aspect of my life my academics, my personal development, my self-confidence, the way I perceive my world everything changed but when I met my husband everything started to change that when I started to accept that even in my adulthood there was second-time assault happened to me before meeting him I kept that abuse too in denial because I didn't want to go through the same pain again and again but slowly I realised accepting what had happened and standing up for myself did wonders to my self-confidence and improved my life.

Table of Contents

PART 1: UNDERSTANDING THE EXPERIENCE

1. Introduction

    - Why This Book Was Written
    - The Universality of Healing: Unisex and Inclusive Perspectives
    - A Note on Trigger Warnings and Self-Care

2. Defining Sexual Abuse

    - What Is Sexual Abuse? (Childhood and Adulthood)
    - Types of Sexual Abuse: Physical, Verbal, Emotional, and Spiritual
    - Recognizing the Signs

3. The Mindset of Abusers

    - What Drives Abusers? Power, Control, and Distorted Thinking
    - Learned Behaviors: The Cycle of Abuse
    - Myths About Abusers (Debunking Stereotypes)

4. The Role of Society in Abuse

    - Cultural and Societal Norms That Perpetuate Silence
    - Victim-Blaming and Stigma: How It Compounds Trauma
    - The Role of Institutions (Family, Religion, Schools,

Workplaces)

PART 2: THE JOURNEY OF RECOVERY

PART 3: TOOLS FOR HEALING

8. Emotional Healing

- Reclaiming Self-Worth
- Emotional Regulation Techniques
- Healing Inner Child Wounds

9. Physical Healing

- Reconnecting with Your Body (Yoga, Exercise, Somatic Therapy)
- Establishing Boundaries and Reclaiming Agency
- Managing Physical Symptoms of Trauma (Sleep, Pain, Fatigue)

10. Spiritual Healing

- Rebuilding Faith in Yourself, Others, or Higher Powers
- Affirmations for Spiritual Empowerment
- Rituals for Cleansing and Renewal

11. The Power of Storytelling

- Using Writing, Art, and Creativity to Process Trauma
- Sharing Your Story to Inspire Others

PART 4: MOVING FORWARD

Appendices

- Resources for Survivors (Books, Websites, Hotlines)
- Trauma-Informed Therapies Explained
- Worksheets for Emotional Processing

Chapter 1: Introduction

Why This Book Was Written

Let's address the elephant in the room: nobody likes talking about sexual abuse. It's like that awkward relative at a family reunion—unavoidable, but everyone pretends it's not there.

Here's the thing: staying silent doesn't make the problem go away. If anything, silence is the perfect fertilizer for abuse to grow unchecked.

When I stood silent in front of my abusers everyone was happy except me I was the only one who was trembling inside with all the shame and the pain but then they didn't realise that they didn't care but it all went downhill for them when I started to voice out what had happened to m.

So, why this book? Because healing shouldn't be a secret recipe you have to decode. It shouldn't feel like stumbling around in the dark, hoping to find the right door. This book is a flashlight—bright, sometimes blunt, but always here to guide you.

This book is for **everyone**.

It's for the person sitting on their bathroom floor, unsure if they can make it through another day. It's for the friend who doesn't know what to say when someone confides in them. It's for the parent, partner, or sibling who wants to understand and support but feels lost.

This isn't some stiff, clinical textbook.

It's not here to overwhelm you with jargon or make you feel like you're sitting in a lecture hall. Think of it as a conversation over coffee (or wine—no judgment). A messy, heartfelt, and even sometimes funny (yes, funny) conversation about a topic that desperately needs light, love, and a whole lot of hope.

Sexual abuse is one of the darkest human experiences, but darkness doesn't stand a chance when we start flipping on the lights.

The Universality of Healing: Unisex and Inclusive Perspectives

Sexual abuse doesn't discriminate. It's an equal-opportunity predator, indifferent to who you are, where you come from, or how much is in your wallet. And yet, society insists on slotting survivors into narrow, predefined boxes.

- Women? Oh yes, of course.
- Men? Hmm, maybe, but let's not talk about it.
- Non-binary or genderqueer individuals? Wait, who?

Let's set the record straight: *anyone can be a survivor*. Abuse doesn't come with a "for women only" label. It doesn't skip over people based on gender, age, or identity. So why do we talk about it like it does?

Alex is a 42-year-old man who was sexually abused as a teenager. For decades, he buried the pain because society told him men aren't victims—they're strong, stoic, and unbreakable. Or consider Taylor, a non-binary individual who felt invisible because the world didn't even have the language to validate their experience.

Healing is for *everyone*. This book is here to smash the stereotypes and make space for every story, every gender, every age. Whether you're a 50-year-old man confronting childhood trauma, a young woman navigating abusive relationships, or someone who doesn't fit neatly into societal boxes, you deserve to heal.

A Note on Trigger Warnings and Self-Care

Let's talk about the big T-word: **triggers**. Healing from trauma isn't a straight path; it's more like an unpredictable rollercoaster. One moment, you're cruising along, thinking, *Hey, I'm doing okay*, and the next, you're plummeting into a loop of overwhelming memories and emotions.

This book isn't here to sugarcoat things. Parts of it might feel heavy, and that's okay. Healing requires looking at the hard stuff, but it also requires knowing when to pause. Think of it like working out: you wouldn't try to lift 200 pounds on your first day at the gym (and if you do, good luck with those sore muscles). The same goes for your emotional muscles.

- **Take Breaks:** If a chapter feels too intense, put it down. Go for a walk. Watch a comedy. Hug your pet (or borrow someone else's).

- **Hydrate:** Yes, this sounds random, but staying hydrated genuinely helps your body process stress. Plus, drinking water is free therapy.
- **Use Grounding Techniques:** If a section hits too close to home, try grounding yourself. Name five things you can see, four you can touch, three you can hear, two you can smell, and one you can taste (even if it's just the stale coffee you forgot about).

This book is like a buffet. Take what you need and leave what you don't. Some parts might feel like they're speaking directly to your soul; others might not resonate at all. That's okay. Healing isn't one-size-fits-all.

What This Book is (and Isn't)

This book isn't a magic wand. It's not going to erase your pain overnight or make everything suddenly okay. But it *is* a roadmap—a guide to help you navigate the messy, complicated, beautiful process of healing.

This book is:

- **Honest:** It won't sugarcoat the hard truths but will always offer hope.
- **Inclusive:** No matter who you are, your story is valid, and your healing matters.
- **Practical:** It's packed with tools, techniques, and insights you can use right away.

What this book *isn't*:

- A substitute for therapy (though it can be a great complement).
- A one-size-fits-all solution.
- A place for judgment or shame.

Why Your Story Matters

Before we dive into the chapters ahead, let's get one thing straight: your story matters. Whether you've spoken it out loud or kept it locked away, it's valid. You are not defined by what happened to you. You are defined by your courage, your resilience, and your decision to seek healing.

Healing isn't about forgetting the past. It's about reclaiming your future. It's about taking back the narrative and deciding that you, not your trauma, are the author of your story.

So, take a deep breath. Grab a notebook if you like to jot things down, or just settle in with an open heart. This isn't just a book—it's a journey, and you're not walking it alone. Let's get started.

Chapter 2: Defining Sexual Abuse

What Is Sexual Abuse? (Childhood and Adulthood)

Let's clear something up right away: sexual abuse isn't just physical acts. It's an abuse of power, trust, and boundaries where someone uses sex or sexuality to harm, manipulate, or control another person. And no, it doesn't have to look like the dramatic courtroom scenes you see on TV. Abuse can be subtle, insidious, and disguised as "harmless."

Sexual abuse can include:

- Unwanted physical contact.
- Coercion or manipulation into sexual acts.
- Verbal harassment or degrading comments.
- Exploiting someone's lack of power or understanding, whether through fear, grooming, or societal pressures.

And here's the kicker: if it feels wrong, it probably is.

Childhood Sexual Abuse:

Childhood abuse often hides under the pretence of trust and authority. It could be a family member who's "too close," a teacher with inappropriate intentions, or a religious figure exploiting their position. Children, being naturally trusting, often don't even realize something is wrong until later in life.

Example: Think of a young girl who's told by a family friend that his "secret tickling game" is just their "special bond." She doesn't understand the boundaries being crossed because she's been groomed to trust him.

Adult Sexual Abuse:

As adults, abuse takes different forms but retains the same power dynamic. It might happen in a romantic relationship where consent is disregarded, in a workplace where a boss uses their authority to exploit, or even in social situations where someone refuses to respect boundaries.

Example: Picture a woman at work who's repeatedly subjected to sexual jokes from her manager. When she complains, she's told to "lighten up" or risk losing her job. This isn't "office banter"—it's abuse.

Sexual abuse doesn't care about age, gender, or social status. It adapts to exploit vulnerabilities in any situation, and understanding this is the first step toward dismantling it.

Types of Sexual Abuse

Sexual abuse wears many disguises, and it's not always the obvious ones we've been conditioned to recognize. Let's break it down:

1. Physical Abuse:

This is what most people think of first—unwanted touching, sexual assault, or rape. It's tangible and visible, but that doesn't make it the only or even the most common form.

Example: A teenage boy is cornered in the locker room by a coach who tells him, "This is how we bond as a team." He feels trapped, humiliated, and powerless to stop it.

2. Verbal Abuse:

Words hurt. When they're laced with objectification, humiliation, or sexual innuendos, they can leave scars that are just as deep as physical ones.

Example: A woman constantly hears lewd comments about her body from a co-worker. Despite asking him to stop, he laughs it off, saying, "It's just a compliment." But it's not—it's harassment.

Why It Hurts: Verbal abuse chips away at self-esteem, making victims feel objectified or unsafe.

3. Emotional Abuse:

Emotional manipulation can make you question your reality, your worth, and your right to say "no." Abusers wield guilt, shame, or fear to control their victims.

Example: A partner insists on a sexual act, saying, "If you really loved me, you'd do this for me." This isn't love—it's coercion disguised as affection.

The Psychological Impact: Emotional abuse often leads to internalized guilt and shame, making it harder for survivors to recognize they've been wronged.

4. Spiritual Abuse:

This one doesn't get talked about enough. Abusers twist spiritual beliefs to justify their actions or silence their victims.

Example: A religious leader tells a survivor that their abuse was "part of God's plan" and insists they forgive their abuser without holding them accountable.

The Harm: Spiritual abuse not only shatters trust in people but also in faith itself, leaving survivors isolated and questioning their beliefs.

Recognizing the Signs

Sexual abuse often comes wrapped in layers of manipulation, guilt, and societal norms, making it hard to identify—even for the survivor. That's why it's crucial to learn the signs:

1. Emotional Signs:

- Feeling constantly anxious or unsafe around a particular person.
- Mood swings, irritability, or unexplained sadness.
- A sudden loss of interest in activities or relationships.

2. Physical Signs:

- Changes in sleep patterns (insomnia or oversleeping).
- Unexplained physical symptoms like fatigue, headaches, or stomach issues—often manifestations of stress and trauma.
- Avoidance of physical contact or flinching at touch.
-

3. Behavioral Signs:

- Withdrawal from loved ones or social activities.

- Acting out, whether through aggression or rebellion.
- Difficulty concentrating or a drop in performance at school or work.

Real-Life Insight:

Meet Liam, a 12-year-old who suddenly stopped wanting to go to soccer practice. His parents thought he was just being moody until he confided that the assistant coach had been making him feel "weird." Listening to his discomfort and trusting his instincts saved him from further harm.

Why Society Struggles to See It

Society often normalizes behaviors that should set off alarm bells. Catcalling? "Just a compliment." A teacher giving special attention? "They just care a lot." A boss making inappropriate jokes? "That's just how he is."

But survivors know better. Abuse thrives in these gray areas, where cultural norms, power dynamics, and misplaced trust intersect. Recognizing abuse means unlearning these harmful patterns and calling out what doesn't sit right.

The Gut Check: Trust Yourself

Here's a rule of thumb: if something feels off, it probably is. Survivors often dismiss their gut instincts because society trains us to second-guess ourselves. But your instincts are powerful—they're your mind and body's way of protecting you.

Questions to Ask Yourself:

- Do I feel safe around this person?
- Are my boundaries being respected?
- Is this behaviour making me feel anxious, uncomfortable, or degraded?

Abuse isn't always loud and obvious. Sometimes it's a whisper, a lingering touch, or a manipulative comment. Trust yourself to recognize it. You're the expert on your own experience.

Summary

Defining sexual abuse is the first step in breaking its cycle. It's not about labelling every uncomfortable situation as abusive but about empowering yourself to recognize what crosses the line. Abuse doesn't have to leave visible scars to be real.

By understanding the forms it takes and trusting your instincts, you take back the power that abuse tries to steal. And with that power, you can begin the journey toward healing and reclaiming your story.

Chapter 3: The Mindset of Abusers

What Drives Abusers? Power, Control, and Distorted Thinking

Here's a hard pill to swallow: sexual abuse isn't about desire—it's about **power**. Abusers are rarely driven by passion or lust. Instead, they are motivated by an overwhelming need for **control** and **dominance**.

They use sex, or any form of abusive behaviour, as a tool to manipulate, dominate, and subjugate their victims. It's not an impulsive act of "passion" — it's calculated, intentional, and cold. They view their victims not as individuals but as objects to control.

Take the example of a teacher who abuses their position of authority by grooming a student. What begins as "special attention" might slowly turn into an abusive dynamic, where the student feels indebted or obligated.

The abuser is not offering affection or care; they're asserting dominance, twisting the relationship to fuel their own needs for power.

Learned Behaviours: The Cycle of Abuse

This is where things get even more complicated. Many abusers were once victims themselves. "Hurt people hurt people" is not just a phrase—it's a grim reality. Abuse often perpetuates across generations, and the scars left by childhood trauma don't magically disappear as people grow older. Instead, they often manifest in behaviours that continue the cycle of harm.

Understanding this doesn't excuse the abuser's actions; no one is absolved of responsibility for their choices. But recognizing that abuse is learned—often by witnessing or experiencing it firsthand—helps explain why it keeps happening.

To break this cycle, we need to address the deeper issues, like generational trauma, rather than just punishing the symptoms. Until the root causes are acknowledged and treated, the cycle will continue.

For example, consider a father who was abused as a child. Growing up in an environment where love was conditional and manipulation was a form of control, he may grow into adulthood emotionally distant, cold, and even manipulative toward his children.

Without intervention, he's more likely to repeat the harmful patterns he experienced, passing on the damage to the next generation.

Myths About Abusers (Debunking Stereotypes)

It's easy to think that abusers fit a certain mould—some dangerous figure lurking in the shadows, or a "bad guy" you can spot from a mile away. But here are a few myths about abusers that need to be shattered:

- **Myth: Abusers are strangers lurking in dark alleys. Reality**: Most abusers are **people we know and trust**. They might be family members, friends, colleagues, or other trusted figures in our lives. The person who abuses has often worked their way into a position of trust, which allows them access to their victims and makes it harder for others to suspect or recognize the abuse.
- **Myth: Abusers are always men. Reality**: **Women and non-binary individuals** can be abusers, too. While male abusers may be more prevalent in certain statistics, it's important to understand that abuse is not gender-exclusive. Anyone can be an abuser, regardless of their gender or identity.
- **Myth: Abusers are easy to spot. Reality**: Many abusers are **charming, well-liked**, and even **respected** members of their communities. They know how to manipulate perceptions, playing the role of a good friend, a reliable colleague, or a caring parent. This charm allows them to gain the trust of others—and, more dangerously, access to their victims.

Abusers are often highly skilled at hiding their true nature behind a facade, making it hard for victims and even the people closest to them to see the warning signs.

This is why it's so important to listen to and support those who speak up, and to never assume that someone is "innocent" just because they seem trustworthy or likable.

The mindset of abusers is rooted in control, distorted thinking, and learned behaviours. Understanding the psychology behind abuse is crucial for breaking the cycle and creating a safer, more supportive environment for everyone.

Chapter 4: The Role of Society in Abuse

Cultural and Societal Norms That Perpetuate Silence

Let's be real for a second: society has an uncanny way of brushing uncomfortable truths under the rug. We've all heard it at some point, whether we're conscious of it or not: "Boys will be boys," or "What was she wearing?"

These phrases aren't just casual comments—they're toxic shortcuts that enable abuse and create a culture of silence.

What's dangerous about these norms is that they *shift the blame*. They minimize or completely ignore the behaviour of abusers, instead focusing on victim-shaming and justifying harmful actions.

It's like a free pass for the abuser to continue their behaviour, while the victim is left to carry the shame and the trauma.

And let's not forget, these excuses can start early. Imagine a teenage girl trying to report harassment at school and being told to "just ignore it," because "boys are like that."

This doesn't just minimize the issue—it invalidates the victim's experience, teaching her that her feelings don't matter and that she's just overreacting.

This normalization of abuse creates an environment where victims feel isolated, confused, and afraid to speak out. It's a cycle that perpetuates itself, year after year, generation after generation.

The issue is that these norms become ingrained in society, and passed on like a bad habit. They shape how we view sexual assault, harassment, and violence.

We're conditioned to dismiss the uncomfortable truth and, in doing so, protect the perpetrators and silence the victims. It's high time we started challenging these norms and creating a culture where survivors feel heard, supported, and believed.

Victim-Blaming and Stigma: How It Compounds Trauma

If you think surviving abuse is bad, imagine surviving it *and then being blamed* for it. That's what happens when society turns a blind eye and starts questioning the survivors instead of supporting them.

Victim blaming is a cruel and insidious form of trauma.

The moment a survivor is met with questions like, "Why didn't you fight back?" or "Why didn't you leave?" they're hit again. First by the abuse, and then by society's judgment.

The abuse itself is horrific enough, but the weight of societal scrutiny can feel even heavier.

It's a sharp reminder that, for some, the survivor's story isn't as important as the *excuse* for the abuser's actions. For instance, a man who was sexually abused may hesitate to report his trauma because he fears the mockery or disbelief that's so often directed toward male victims.

Society has a limited and stereotypical view of abuse: women are the victims, and men are the perpetrators.

This narrative makes it even harder for male survivors to come forward. They fear being dismissed, laughed at, or worse—accused of lying or exaggerating. This stigma prevents many from finding support, leaving them isolated with their pain.

But victim-blaming doesn't just affect men. It affects people of all genders and backgrounds. Survivors from marginalized groups, such as LGBTQIA+ individuals, often face an added layer of stigma, where their abuse may be ignored or invalidated due to biases or prejudices.

The more society continues to blame the victim, the harder it becomes to break free from the cycle of silence and shame.

If we want real change, we need to start holding abusers accountable and creating a culture where survivors are not only believed but *supported* in their healing journey.

The Role of Institutions (Family, Religion, Schools, Workplaces)

Institutions—family, religion, schools, workplaces—should be places where survivors can seek help and find refuge.

Instead, they're often where abuse is ignored or even *enabled*. Institutions hold incredible power; they can either serve as a lifeline for survivors or act as a barrier that keeps them trapped in silence.

The problem is that many institutions, driven by their own interests and a desire to preserve their reputation, choose to protect the abuser over the victim.

Take the family dynamic, for example. It's common for families to deny or downplay abuse to "keep the peace." No one wants to be the one to rock the boat, especially if it involves a close family member or someone well-regarded in the community.

A child may tell a parent about abuse, only to have the parent brush it off or try to protect the abuser for the sake of family harmony. This denial of reality not only fails the victim—it often reinforces the belief that abuse is something to be kept secret, something to be ashamed of.

In schools, the situation can be just as dangerous. When a survivor reports abuse, the institution's priority often shifts to preserving the reputation of the school or protecting star athletes.

A victim might report sexual harassment or assault only to be told to "move on" or "not make a scene," while the perpetrator, who might be an athlete or popular student, receives minimal consequences.

This prioritization of image over justice allows abuse to continue unchecked. It silences the voices of those who need support the most.

Even in places of worship, where one would expect safety and guidance, abuse can be swept under the rug. Consider the case of a church prioritizing the reputation of an abuser over the safety of their congregation. This happens more often than we'd like to believe—abusers are sometimes protected because of their position in the church, or because the institution fears losing followers or financial support.

The church's reputation becomes more important than the well-being of its members. For many survivors, this betrayal can be one of the hardest to bear—especially when the very institution they trusted to guide them is the one that lets them down.

Why Society Must Do Better

Ultimately, the role of society in abuse is one of complicit silence. Whether it's family, religion, schools, or workplaces, institutions that are supposed to protect often fail the very people they are meant to serve. And when society dismisses, blames, or invalidates survivors, the cycle of abuse only continues.

If we want to truly make a difference, it's essential to challenge these norms, debunk harmful myths, and demand accountability from institutions. We need to create a world where survivors are believed, supported, and empowered to come forward.

Breaking the silence is the first step toward healing—not just for the individual survivor, but for society as a whole. It's time we stop hiding from uncomfortable truths and start supporting the change that needs to happen.

Chapter 5: Breaking the Silence

Finding the Courage to Acknowledge Abuse

Let's get real: acknowledging abuse is one of the hardest things anyone can do. It's not like flipping a switch or finding an easy way out.

It feels like opening a can of worms you've kept tightly sealed for years—except it's not worms; it's the full, raw, unprocessed mess of emotions, memories, and confusion.

You might wonder, *What if no one believes me? What if I'm just overreacting? What if it was my fault?* These questions are normal. But here's the thing: those thoughts are not truths. They are the lies that abuse plants in your head to keep you small, scared, and silent.

Acknowledging what happened doesn't have to be some grand public declaration. It doesn't mean shouting your story from the rooftops or telling every person you meet.

It can be as quiet and personal as simply whispering it to yourself: *This happened. It wasn't okay. And it wasn't my fault.* That's your starting point.

It might feel like the first step toward a mountain, but each small step you take is a victory. Remember: you don't need to have it all figured out right away. Just acknowledging the truth of your experience is an act of incredible strength.

Why It's So Hard to Acknowledge Abuse

It's no secret that facing abuse head-on is incredibly difficult. There are layers of shame, doubt, and fear to peel away, each one making the task feel like an uphill battle. Let's break down why this is so tough:

1. **Fear of Judgment**: Society loves to judge. From the moment abuse is mentioned, people start to weigh in. "What were you wearing?" "Why didn't you speak up sooner?"

These kinds of questions are not only hurtful, they also create a narrative that *you* are somehow to blame. No one should have to endure judgment for something they didn't cause.

1. **Self-Doubt**: When abuse happens, the lines between what's acceptable and what's not can get blurry, especially if the abuser is someone you know or trust.

You might ask yourself, *Was that really abuse?* Spoiler alert: if it hurt you—physically, emotionally, or mentally—it counts. Don't let anyone, not even your own mind, convince you otherwise.

1. **Emotional Overload**: Acknowledging abuse often brings a flood of emotions: anger, shame, guilt, sadness, and confusion.

It can feel like your entire emotional world is being tossed around in a whirlwind, and facing all of it at once can be overwhelming. But you don't need to do it all in one go. Take it slow, one moment at a time.

Here's the thing: You don't need to go through this alone, and you don't need to dive into it all at once. It's okay to take small, manageable steps. Write about it in a journal, talk to someone you trust, or even say it out loud in the mirror. Every time you take a step forward, your courage will grow.

Sharing Your Story Safely (When, How, and With Whom)

Okay, so you're ready to talk. That's huge. But now the question is: Who do you tell? This isn't about opening up to just anyone or blurting it out to the first person you see. This is about finding a safe space where you can share without fear of judgment or invalidation. So, how do you choose your listener wisely?

1. **Choose Wisely**: Look for someone you trust—someone who will listen without jumping to conclusions, offering unsolicited advice, or making it about themselves. A good friend, a therapist, a support group, or a compassionate family member might be the right choice. Avoid people who have a history of dismissing or minimizing your feelings. Your healing journey deserves respect.
2. **Set Boundaries**: When you share your story, make it clear what you need from the conversation. If you're just looking for someone to listen, say that upfront: *"I'm not looking for advice right now; I just need someone to listen."* Setting clear expectations helps prevent misunderstandings and allows the conversation to focus on *you*, not on fixing things immediately.
3. **Prepare for Mixed Reactions**: Not everyone will respond the way you hope. Some may be supportive, offering comfort and understanding. Others might freeze up or become awkward,

unsure how to react. That's okay. Their reaction is about them, not you. Your healing doesn't depend on how others respond, but rather on how *you* choose to move forward. The people who truly care about you will stand by your side—don't let a few awkward moments deter you from finding those who will help you heal.

Real-Life Example:

Imagine sitting down with a close friend and telling them your story. There's a chance they'll listen intently, their face showing empathy. "I had no idea. Thank you for trusting me," they might say. That's the response you want—support, kindness, and validation.

But there's also a chance they might freeze up, unable to process what you're saying, or they might quickly change the subject to something safer. It's disappointing, and it might even feel like a rejection. But remember: that's on *them*. It's not a reflection of your worth or your story. It's a sign that they might not be equipped to handle it right now. That's okay. Your healing journey isn't dependent on their reaction. It's about you finding your strength and creating a support system that *does* lift you up.

Navigating Reactions from Others

Let's talk about the tough part—how people will react when you share your truth.

Spoiler alert: not everyone will respond well. Some people may doubt you. Some may minimize your experience. And some may even defend the abuser. It's heartbreaking, and it can feel like another layer of rejection, but here's the thing: *It's not your responsibility to change their mind.*

Here's a breakdown of common reactions and how to handle them:

1. **Supportive Response**: "Thank you for sharing. How can I help?"
    - **Response:** Lean on these people. They're your allies. Accept

their support, and let them help you in whatever way feels right. These are the people who will walk with you through this journey.

2. **Dismissive Response**: "Are you sure it was that bad?"
   - **Response**: It's important to set boundaries. Firmly say, *"I need support, not doubt."* You don't have to convince anyone of your experience. You deserve to be believed, and if someone can't offer that, they're not the person you need right now.
3. **Angry Response**: "Why didn't you tell me sooner?"
   - **Response**: Stay calm and explain, if you're comfortable: *"I wasn't ready to share this until now."* People may feel hurt or confused that you didn't come forward earlier, but remember: your timeline is yours to control. Healing happens in your own time.

In the end, sharing your story is about *you*—your healing, your journey, and your voice. Focus on your recovery, not on how others react. People who truly care will support you, and those who don't? Well, that's just a part of the process. Let their reactions roll off your back as you continue to heal and move forward.

Chapter 6: Understanding the Impact of Abuse

Physical and Emotional Effects

Abuse leaves scars that aren't always visible to the naked eye. While physical wounds might heal, the trauma lives on in the body and mind in ways you often don't realize until much later. The damage isn't just skin-deep—it's emotional, mental, and physical, affecting every part of your being.

Emotional Effects:

1. **Shame and Guilt**
   Survivors often carry an overwhelming sense of shame and guilt, even when they had no control over what happened. They might wonder, *Was it something I did? Could I have stopped it?* Here's the painful truth: *it wasn't your fault.* But the impact of the abuse is so profound that it convinces you otherwise. Abuse convinces you that you are unworthy or deserving of what happened, and that toxic belief can take root deeply within you.

Imagine a survivor blaming themselves for not speaking out sooner, or feeling shameful for things beyond their control—like not resisting an abuser's actions. It's important to recognize that this self-blame is not reality; it's an illusion created by the abuser's manipulation and the shame society places on survivors. You didn't ask for this, and you certainly didn't deserve it.

1. **Anxiety and Depression**
   Abuse has a way of rewiring the brain, making fear, sadness, and hopelessness feel like the baseline emotions. Anxiety can become constant, lingering in the background of every

thought, every decision. Depression might take root, leaving a survivor feeling numb, exhausted, or detached from life. These emotions aren't just feelings—they're biological responses to trauma. Your body and brain have been altered by what you've endured, making it harder to feel joy or safety in the present.

Survivors might feel like they're constantly on edge, unable to relax, unable to trust that the world is safe. This anxiety doesn't just come from nowhere; it's a direct consequence of the chaos and unpredictability caused by abuse.
It's an emotional burden that lingers, sometimes without explanation, as if the world is a dangerous place, and they are still trapped in it.

1. **Trust Issues**
   When someone close to you betrays your trust—whether it's an intimate partner, a family member, or someone in authority—it can feel like the foundation of your reality has been shattered. Trust becomes something fragile, something you can never fully rebuild.

If someone you depended on violated your boundaries or exploited your vulnerability, trusting others, even those who care about you, becomes terrifying.

Trust issues aren't just about paranoia or scepticism; they're rooted in deep emotional pain. The survivor might feel as if their judgment was flawed, or question whether they can ever trust their perceptions again. This is a normal response, but it doesn't have to last forever. With time, therapy, and self-compassion, it's possible to learn to trust again—but it's a process, and it takes patience.
Physical Effects:

1. **Chronic Pain and Fatigue**

Abuse doesn't just affect your mind—it often manifests physically. Survivors may experience chronic pain, fatigue, or other unexplained symptoms that seem to have no clear cause.

2. This can include muscle tension, headaches, digestive issues, or even autoimmune responses. It's as if the body carries the burden of the trauma, storing it in physical form.

The body holds onto what the mind may not always be able to process. For some survivors, this constant physical discomfort can be a reminder of their pain, even if they aren't consciously aware of it. This is why it's important to address both physical and emotional aspects of healing.

1. **Trouble Sleeping and Nightmares**
   A disrupted sleep cycle is common for many survivors. Nightmares, insomnia, or restless sleep can be the body's way of processing trauma. Sleep can become a battlefield, with the mind replaying past events or creating terrifying scenarios that feel just as real as the abuse itself. Survivors may avoid sleep because it feels like they're reliving the trauma or losing control.

Restoring a healthy sleep routine is crucial for recovery. But it's not as simple as just "getting more rest" because the trauma itself disrupts the body's ability to relax fully.

1. **"Frozen" Body Response**
   Many survivors experience a sort of constant tension, a sense that their body is always on high alert. The muscles are tight, the mind is tense, and there's little ability to relax fully. This hypervigilance is a response to the unpredictability of abuse. The body stays in "fight or flight" mode, even after the danger has passed. It's a physical manifestation of living in survival mode for too long.

Healing requires learning to release that tension—whether through physical therapy, mindfulness, yoga, or other calming practices. It's about teaching the body to trust again, to let go of the constant readiness for danger.

Science Speaks:

The body *remembers* trauma. Research has shown that abuse can impact the brain's key areas—specifically, the amygdala (the part of the brain responsible for processing fear) and the prefrontal cortex (the part responsible for decision-making). This means that survivors might find themselves overreacting to small triggers or struggling to concentrate. It's not because they're weak or overdramatic; it's because their brain has been rewired to expect danger, even when there is none.

This is why some survivors might jump at loud noises or become easily startled by seemingly innocent events. Their body is reacting as if the danger is still present, even though it's not. Understanding this physical response helps reduce self-blame because it's a *biological reaction* to trauma, not a sign of weakness.

Real-Life Example:

Let's say you're at a café, and a loud crash happens nearby. Without thinking, you jump or freeze. Your heart races. Your breath quickens. You're suddenly back in a moment of fear, not even realizing that your body is reliving past danger.

Your brain is responding to the trigger, not to the present situation. Understanding that this is your body's trauma response can help you be kinder to yourself. You're not overreacting; you're surviving.

The Long-Term Effects of Childhood vs. Adult Sexual Abuse

The impact of abuse changes depending on when it occurs in your life—during childhood or adulthood—and both are equally valid and significant.

1. **Childhood Abuse:**

   When abuse happens during childhood, it can alter the very

way the brain develops. A child's sense of self, their understanding of relationships, and their ability to feel loved and valued are all affected. Survivors of childhood abuse might struggle with their identity or feel unworthy of love, even though those beliefs are lies created by the abuse.

For example, a child abused by a caregiver might grow up believing they are unlovable or that they are destined to be treated poorly in relationships. These beliefs can follow them into adulthood, causing difficulty in forming healthy relationships or in valuing themselves.

1. **Adult Abuse:**
   Adult survivors of abuse often face a different but equally painful struggle. For adults, the abuse might shatter their sense of autonomy, self-worth, and trust in others. They may question their judgment, especially if the abuse took place in a close, trusted relationship. This can make it difficult to enter new relationships or take risks in life.

For example, an adult survivor of workplace harassment might avoid new opportunities for fear of facing similar abuse again. Their confidence is shaken, and their belief in their ability to make sound decisions is undermined. It's important to remember that the pain might look different depending on age, but the journey toward healing is just as valid.

How Trauma Manifests in the Mind and Body

Trauma doesn't just disappear after the event is over. It lingers—often in the form of physical and mental manifestations that can be triggered by the smallest things. Here are a few examples of how trauma can affect you:

1. **Flashbacks**: These are moments where it feels like the abuse is happening all over again. A flashback isn't just remembering

what happened; it's *re-living* it, as if it's happening in real time. It's intense and disorienting.

2. **Dissociation**: Sometimes, the mind checks out to avoid the pain. Dissociation is a way for the brain to protect itself from overwhelming emotions. You might feel disconnected from your body, like you're watching yourself from the outside, or as if things aren't real.
3. **Physical Symptoms**: The body can react to trauma in unexpected ways—stomachaches, migraines, chronic pain, or unexplained fatigue. These physical symptoms are ways your body is holding onto emotional pain.

Real-Life Example:

Imagine you're walking into a store and the smell of cologne hits you. It immediately makes you tense up, and your stomach churns. You don't realize it, but that scent might be connected to a past traumatic event—something that your brain associates with danger. Understanding these physical responses is the first step in healing. You're not weak, you're human. And your body is simply trying to protect you.

Chapter 7: The Path to Forgiveness (or Not)

What Forgiveness Means (And Doesn't Mean)

Forgiveness. It's a word that gets tossed around a lot in the healing process like it's some magical key that will unlock your peace and make everything better. But here's the truth—it's not.

Forgiveness is optional. You do *not* have to forgive your abuser to heal, and that's okay. The idea that you must forgive to move on can feel like another burden when you're already carrying so much weight.

Forgiveness is not a one-size-fits-all, and it's not a mandatory box to check on the healing checklist.

It's personal, it's complex, and it's up to *you* whether it feels right. You can still rebuild your life and reclaim your joy without ever saying, *"I forgive you"* to the person who hurt you.

What Forgiveness Isn't:

1. **Excusing the Abuse**
   Forgiveness isn't about pretending the abuse didn't happen or saying, *"It wasn't so bad."* You don't have to make excuses for someone who violated your trust or caused you harm. Forgiving them doesn't mean you minimize the pain or accept their behavior as "just a part of life."

It simply means you're taking back the power they've stolen by refusing to stay trapped in the anger or resentment they left behind.

1. **Forgetting What Happened**
   Forgetting the abuse is unrealistic. And let's be real, it wouldn't really be helpful either. Healing doesn't require erasure.

What's far more empowering is *remembering*, and in doing so, acknowledging your strength, your resilience, and your survival. The goal isn't to forget—it's to process what happened, understand it, and then move forward without the abuse ruling your life.

1. **Rebuilding a Relationship with the Abuser**
   You can forgive and still choose to keep your distance. Forgiveness doesn't mean you have to rebuild a relationship with the person who harmed you.

For many survivors, keeping them out of your life—cutting them out entirely—is an important part of reclaiming your boundaries and power.

This might be hard for some to accept, but *you* decide who gets access to your energy, your time, and your life. And sometimes, that means leaving the abuser in the past, where they belong.

What Forgiveness Can Be:

1. **Releasing the Hold the Abuser Has on Your Emotions**
   If forgiveness feels like something that would help you, think of it like this: it's not for them—it's for you. It's about *taking back control* of your emotions and not letting the anger, sadness, or resentment hold you hostage anymore. You don't have to forget or forgive them to do this—you simply have to decide that the pain they caused you won't define your future. Forgiveness, in this case, is about setting yourself free from their influence on your life.
2. **Finding Peace for Yourself, Not Them**
   The biggest misconception about forgiveness is that it's somehow for the abuser like it's a gift you give them. It's not. If forgiveness is something you choose, it's for *your* peace, your mental health, and your well-being.

It's about *you* finding closure. You're not letting them off the hook—you're just choosing to stop letting their actions dictate your happiness. You're freeing yourself from their shadow, so you can stand tall in the light of your own life.

If forgiving feels right for you, then do it on your own terms. If it doesn't, that's okay too. Healing doesn't need forgiveness to be valid, and there's no timeline for how or when it should happen. It's your journey, and you are the one in control of it.

Forgiving Yourself: Letting Go of Shame and Guilt

Now let's talk about the most important kind of forgiveness—the one that *only* you can give: self-forgiveness. This is where the real work begins. Because here's the deal—abuse is *never* your fault. Yet so many survivors find themselves weighed down by a heavy backpack full of shame, guilt, and regret. It's time to put that backpack down.

Self-forgiveness often feels like the hardest thing to offer yourself. After everything you've been through, it can feel like you should have *done something, said something, fought back*, or *left sooner*. But here's the brutal truth: you did what you needed to survive. The fact that you survived is a testament to your strength.

In those moments, when you were caught in the chaos of abuse, *you* did what you had to do to keep yourself as safe as possible. It's not about being perfect. It's about surviving. And you did that. You're a survivor, not a failure.

Tips for Self-Forgiveness:

1. **Challenge Negative Thoughts**
   When those toxic, self-blaming thoughts creep in—*Why didn't I stop it? Why didn't I just leave?*—pause and challenge them. What would you say to a friend in the same situation? You wouldn't tell them they're stupid or weak.

You'd tell them they did the best they could under impossible circumstances. So why not show yourself the same compassion? Replace those negative thoughts with, *I did the best I could in a terrible situation.* Your past choices don't define your worth—they were survival tactics, not failures.

1. **Write Yourself a Letter**
   Sometimes, the most powerful tool is simply writing. Write a

letter to yourself, from a place of deep compassion. Pour out all the things you need to hear—the words of kindness, understanding, and love. Imagine telling yourself exactly what you'd tell a friend who's been through the same experience. Remind yourself that you are worthy of love, that you didn't deserve what happened, and that your feelings matter. You need to hear this, even if no one else ever says it to you.

2. **Practice Self-Compassion**
   Many survivors are far more compassionate toward others than they are toward themselves. It's time to change that. Treat yourself with the same care, kindness, and understanding that you'd show to someone you love deeply. You've been through so much—don't add more weight by being hard on yourself. You survived, and that's what matters. You deserve healing, and you deserve kindness. You owe it to yourself to practice self-compassion every single day.

Real-Life Example:
Imagine this: a survivor replays the abuse over and over in their mind, asking themselves, *Why didn't I fight back? Why didn't I leave sooner?* But here's the truth: when you're in a traumatic situation, your brain doesn't always function "normally." You might freeze, dissociate, or go into survival mode.

Your body is doing everything it can to protect you. *It's not about being perfect—it's about surviving.* When you look back, don't berate yourself. Instead, remember that in that moment, you were doing everything you could just to make it through.

If you could go back in time and talk to yourself, you wouldn't criticize yourself for not being "stronger" or "better." You'd reassure yourself that you were doing the best you could under circumstances that were impossible to control. You were human, and sometimes, being human means not being perfect—and that's okay.

Forgiveness doesn't mean erasing the pain, the anger, or the memories. It means *reclaiming control* over them. It means setting down the shame, guilt, and "what ifs" so you can move forward in freedom.

If forgiveness feels right for you, great—but if it doesn't, that's equally valid. Your healing journey doesn't need to follow any prescribed timeline. What matters is that you move forward, however that looks for you. You are enough, and your healing will unfold exactly as it needs to, in your own time and on your own terms.

Chapter 8: Emotional Healing

Reclaiming Self-Worth

One of the most insidious effects of abuse is the way it can make you feel like you're not enough—like you're broken beyond repair. You might hear a voice in your head saying, *I'm unlovable. I'll never be good enough. I'll always be broken.*

Let's be clear: *that voice is a liar.* Abuse isn't just an attack on your body or your safety; it's an attack on your self-worth, making you question your value and your ability to be loved or cared for.

Here's the thing: abusers often project their insecurities onto their victims, making you believe that something is wrong with *you* when the truth is, the problem was never yours. You were never broken. You were never the problem.

Reclaiming your self-worth is about rejecting the lies you were told and remembering that you are worthy of love, respect, and care. It's about finding the real you underneath all the layers of shame, guilt, and self-doubt that abuse may have left behind.

Science Speaks:

The brain is wired with a "negativity bias," which means we're more likely to remember and focus on the bad stuff, the critical stuff, than the good stuff. That's why abuse can leave such a lasting mark. But here's some good news: *neuroscience* tells us that the brain is also incredibly adaptable. You can rewire it over time through practices like self-affirmations and gratitude. It's like reprogramming a computer. So, while those negative thoughts might feel like they have control now, you can fight back and take back your power.

Tools to Rebuild Self-Worth

1. **Affirmations**
   It might feel awkward or even downright cheesy at first, but one of the simplest ways to start rebuilding your self-worth is through *affirmations.* Stand in front of the mirror, look yourself in the eyes, and say something like, "I am enough." Start small, and don't worry if you don't believe it right away. Repetition is key. The more you say it, the more your brain starts to accept it. Think of it like planting seeds in your mind—they might not sprout immediately, but with time, they'll grow.
2. **Self-Compassion Exercises**
   Imagine a friend—someone you care about deeply—telling you they feel worthless. How would you respond? Would you judge them? Would you tell them they're not good enough? *Of course not.* You'd offer them love, kindness, and support. Now, turn that compassion toward yourself. You deserve the same tenderness and care you would give a loved one. Practicing self-compassion is like rebuilding a safe space within yourself—one where you can heal and grow.

Emotional Regulation Techniques

After abuse, it's completely normal to feel like your emotions are on a rollercoaster—one minute you're angry, the next you're deeply sad or fearful, and then you might feel shame creeping in. All of these emotions are valid. But the intensity of them can be overwhelming, and learning to manage them is crucial to healing. Think of it like learning to ride wild horses—emotions can be untamed, but with some practice, you can learn how to stay in control.

Techniques to Try:

1. **Deep Breathing**
   One of the simplest ways to calm your mind and body is deep breathing. Try this: Inhale slowly for a count of four, hold the breath for four, and then exhale for six. The exhale is important because it triggers your parasympathetic nervous system (the "rest and digest" part of your nervous system), helping your body relax and your mind to settle. It's a quick and easy way to regain some control when your emotions feel like they're spiraling.
2. **Label Your Emotions**
   Sometimes, emotions can feel like a cloud of confusion. You know something's off, but it's hard to pinpoint exactly what. Try labeling your feelings—say them out loud, even if no one is around. "I'm angry," "I'm sad," or "I'm anxious." This simple act helps activate your prefrontal cortex (the part of the brain that helps you process emotions), which allows you to step outside of the emotion and observe it without letting it consume you.
3. **Grounding Exercises**
   Grounding exercises are about reconnecting with the present moment and reminding yourself that you are safe, right here, right now. One common grounding technique is the "5-4-3-2-1" method. Name 5 things you see around you, 4 things you can feel, 3 things you can hear, 2 things you can smell, and 1 thing you can taste. This exercise helps bring your focus away from overwhelming emotions and back to the world around you.

Real-Life Example:

Imagine you're in a crowded room, feeling overwhelmed, like your heart is racing and your chest is tightening. You step outside, close your eyes, and take a few deep breaths. As you focus on your breathing, you start labeling your emotions: "I'm feeling anxiety right now." Just by identifying what's happening, you begin to feel more in control, like you're no longer just a passenger in your own body.

Healing Inner Child Wounds

The "inner child" is the part of you that experienced the abuse—the child who was scared, confused, and vulnerable. Healing your inner child is like going back in time and offering them the safety, love, and protection they never received. Think of it as re-parenting yourself with the care and nurturing you deserved back then.

Ways to Heal Your Inner Child:

1. **Visualization**
   One powerful tool for healing your inner child is visualization. Picture yourself as a young child—maybe around the age when the abuse began. Imagine yourself running to your younger self, wrapping them in a hug, and saying, "You're safe now. You're loved. You're enough." This simple act of connecting with your inner child can bring a sense of comfort and reassurance. It's a reminder that *you* are the protector now.
2. **Creative Play**
   Revisit some of the activities you enjoyed as a child—things like painting, singing, playing with Legos, or dancing around your room. It might seem silly or childish, but this kind of play is deeply healing. It allows you to reconnect with the joy, curiosity, and innocence of your younger self. It also lets you nurture that part of you in a way that wasn't possible before.
3. **Reparenting**
   Reparenting is about giving yourself the care and love you needed back then. It's about setting boundaries for yourself,

recognizing your worth, and seeking therapy or support when needed. Reparenting means *taking care* of yourself now, the way a loving, supportive parent would. It might also mean offering yourself compassion when you make mistakes and celebrating yourself when you achieve things. This is how you build a new foundation of safety, love, and respect.

Psychological Insight:
Inner child work taps into the subconscious, the part of your mind where much of your trauma is stored. By engaging with your inner child, you're not only healing those old wounds—you're also rewiring your brain, creating new pathways for self-love and self-care. It's like planting seeds for a healthier future.

Healing from abuse isn't linear, and it isn't easy. But with the right tools and mindset, it's absolutely possible to reclaim your sense of self-worth, regulate your emotions, and heal those deep wounds from the past. The process can be messy and imperfect, but it's also powerful and transformative. And remember: You're not alone in this journey. Healing is a deeply personal process, and however it unfolds for you, it's exactly how it's meant to be.

Chapter 9: Physical Healing

Reconnecting with Your Body

One of the toughest things abuse can do is sever the connection you have with your body. Abuse often leaves survivors feeling like their bodies betrayed them or like they don't belong in their own skin. You might even feel like your body isn't really yours to control, or you might feel numb to it altogether. Reconnecting with your body is a vital part of healing—it's about taking back ownership and agency, about reclaiming the right to feel and experience life through your own body again.

The first step in reconnecting with your body is learning to listen to it. For so long, your body may have been something you were trying to escape, but healing comes from recognizing it as the tool that kept you alive and now has the potential to help you thrive.

Here are some methods that can help you begin the journey of reconnecting with your body:

1. Yoga

Yoga can be a powerful way to reclaim your physical self. Trauma-focused yoga is especially gentle and focuses on creating a safe, nurturing environment. Unlike traditional yoga, which may emphasize flexibility and strength, trauma-informed yoga teaches you to approach your body with compassion. It encourages mindfulness and breathwork, which can help you reconnect with yourself at a pace that feels comfortable. For survivors, yoga can help release trauma stored in the body and gradually bring back a sense of safety.

In trauma-informed yoga, the focus isn't on performing the poses perfectly—it's about listening to your body and finding a flow that feels right for you. Some survivors may find it hard to relax in certain poses at first—like child's pose, which can bring up feelings of vulnerability—but over time, with patience and practice, yoga can help you feel more grounded and at home in your body.

2. Somatic Therapy

Somatic therapy is all about tuning into the sensations in your body. After trauma, you may find that your body holds onto emotional pain in subtle (and sometimes not-so-subtle) ways. Somatic therapy helps you become aware of these sensations and use them to process emotions that may have been trapped inside. By focusing on how your body feels—whether it's tension in your shoulders, tightness in your chest, or a racing heartbeat—you can start to understand how emotions like fear, anger, or sadness manifest physically.

Somatic therapy invites you to explore these sensations with curiosity rather than fear, allowing you to heal on a deeper, more holistic level. You'll be learning to tune back into your body in a way that feels empowering rather than overwhelming.

3. Dance

Sometimes, the most liberating thing you can do is to *move*. Dance can be incredibly healing for survivors, even if you don't consider yourself a dancer. It's not about perfect choreography or "looking good." It's about freedom, expression, and reconnecting with the joy of movement. Dancing to music—whether in your living room, at a club, or in a safe, private space—can be a profound way to release pent-up emotions and restore agency to your body. When you dance, you're allowing your body to express itself without judgement, reclaiming its natural rhythm and flow.

Real-Life Example:

A survivor might walk into a yoga class for the first time and feel immediately uncomfortable, especially in poses that require vulnerability, like child's pose, where you're crouching and tucking your body. It may feel like too much at first. But with time, as they practice mindfulness and focus on their breath, they begin to notice a shift. Their body doesn't feel like an enemy anymore—it feels like a safe space. Little by little, they reclaim the space they've been missing. The more they connect with their breath and movement, the more they reconnect with the strength and resilience their body has always had.

Establishing Boundaries and Reclaiming Agency

After experiencing abuse, setting boundaries might feel impossible. You may feel like you've lost control of your life, your body, and your space. However, boundaries are one of the most empowering tools you have. They are the lines that protect you, the fences that say, "This is where I end and where you begin." Boundaries help you restore your sense of self and agency, ensuring that you have control over who gets access to your time, your energy, and your body.

Learning to set boundaries isn't easy, but it is a crucial step in reclaiming your sense of self-worth and autonomy. At first, boundaries might feel uncomfortable, especially if you've spent years ignoring your own needs in favor of others. But over time, boundaries will help you honor your needs and protect your peace.

Tips for Setting Boundaries:

1. **Start Small**
   If the idea of setting boundaries feels overwhelming, start with small, manageable steps. Practice saying "no" to things that don't feel right—whether it's a request for your time, your energy, or your emotional labor. It could be as simple as saying no to a social event when you're not feeling up to it. Boundaries don't have to be big declarations—they can start with small acts of self-respect.
2. **Use "I" Statements**
   When setting boundaries, it's helpful to use "I" statements. Instead of saying, "You're making me uncomfortable," try saying, "I feel uncomfortable when this happens." This shifts the focus from the other person's behavior to your own feelings, which helps communicate your needs more clearly and without aggression.
3. **Expect Pushback**
   Here's a hard truth: some people won't respect your

boundaries. They might resist, try to manipulate you, or push you to go against your needs. But your boundaries are yours to keep. Even if people push back, hold firm. Your peace, your energy, and your safety matter more than their discomfort.

Psychological Insight:
Boundaries are more than just a way to protect yourself—they also teach your brain that you're in control again. After trauma, we often feel helpless, like we don't have power over our own lives. But boundaries can help reduce those feelings of helplessness by reminding you that you have control over your own space, time, and energy. Setting boundaries reinforces the idea that you are the one who decides what's acceptable in your life.

Managing Physical Symptoms of Trauma

Trauma isn't just a mental experience—it also shows up in the body. Chronic pain, insomnia, fatigue, and even gastrointestinal issues are common among survivors. These physical symptoms can be a direct result of trauma, as your body holds onto stress and pain from the past. Healing isn't just about addressing the emotional and psychological impacts—it's also about taking care of your body and helping it heal from the physical aftermath of trauma.

Tips for Physical Healing:

1. **Sleep Hygiene**
   Good sleep is crucial for healing, but trauma can make restful sleep elusive. Establishing a bedtime routine can help signal to your body that it's time to relax. Avoid screens and bright lights before bed, and try incorporating calming rituals, like reading or taking a warm bath. If anxiety is a major issue, consider using a weighted blanket, which can offer a sense of comfort and security.
2. **Pain Management**
   Trauma often leaves a physical imprint on the body, like

chronic pain. Gentle exercise, like walking or stretching, can help release tension and promote circulation. Massage therapy can also help relieve muscle tightness, and acupuncture has been shown to support the body's healing process. You don't have to live with pain. There are many ways to find relief.

3. **Nutrition**

   Nutrition plays a huge role in physical healing. Eating balanced, nourishing meals can support your body as it recovers from the effects of trauma. Focus on whole foods—fruits, vegetables, lean proteins, and healthy fats—and make sure you're staying hydrated. Your body needs fuel to heal, and taking care of your physical health through nutrition is a vital part of that process.

Real-Life Example:

A survivor with chronic back pain might start somatic therapy and discover that their tension stems from years of holding in fear. They realize that the tightness in their back isn't just physical—it's tied to emotional pain they've been holding onto for years. As they learn to release these emotions, they notice the pain in their back starts to ease. Over time, they find that emotional healing and physical healing go hand in hand.

Healing is a holistic journey, and physical healing is just as important as emotional or psychological recovery. Reconnecting with your body, setting boundaries, and managing physical symptoms are all essential steps toward reclaiming your agency and your peace. It's not an easy process, but with patience, compassion, and the right tools, you can rebuild your strength, your health, and your life. You deserve to feel at home in your body again. You deserve to feel whole.

Chapter 10: Spiritual Healing

Rebuilding Faith in Yourself, Others, or Higher Powers

When you've been through abuse, it can shake your sense of trust—not just in others, but in yourself, your ability to heal, and sometimes, even in something larger than yourself, like God, the universe, or the simple rhythms of life. Spirituality can mean a lot of things, and it can take many forms. For some, it's tied to a specific religious faith; for others, it's about finding a deep connection to nature, to art, or to the quiet moments in between. Rebuilding faith, then, is personal—it's not about fitting yourself into someone else's mold but about finding your own path back to what feels grounding, inspiring, and authentic for you.

After trauma, it's easy to feel lost, like you don't know what or who you can trust anymore. But spirituality can offer a safe space to rebuild that trust, whether it's by reclaiming faith in yourself, in others, or in a higher power. It's about reconnecting with something bigger than the pain, something that can help carry you through the tough times. Here's how you can begin:

Ways to Reconnect Spiritually:

1. Nature

Sometimes, the most profound spiritual experiences don't happen in church or temples—they happen in the quiet moments outdoors. There's something incredibly healing about being in nature, away from the noise of the world, and reconnecting with the rhythm of the earth. Nature doesn't judge you. The trees don't care about your past, and the stars don't hold your pain against you. They just are. Whether it's a walk through the park, sitting by the ocean, or hiking up a mountain trail, being in nature can help you tap into something larger than yourself, grounding you and reminding you that life is cyclical. The seasons change. The sun rises and sets. Life keeps going, and so can you.

2. Meditation

Meditation is like a reset button for your mind. It helps you quiet the noise and find peace within yourself. This isn't about "emptying your mind"—it's about creating space to breathe, to be still, and to check in with yourself. There are many ways to meditate, and you don't have to sit in the lotus position for hours to get the benefits. You can start with focusing on your breath for a few minutes each day. Some people use mantras, repeating words like "peace" or "I am safe" to bring calm. Others focus on a candle flame, a sound, or even a feeling of warmth. Whatever it is, meditation can help you reconnect with your center and find strength in stillness.

3. Faith Communities

If you've been part of a spiritual or religious community in the past, you might feel disconnected from that world after trauma. Abuse can make you question everything you once believed, but faith doesn't have to be all or nothing. If it feels right for you, reconnecting with a faith community or spiritual practice might help you rebuild a sense of belonging. Whether it's attending a service, joining a study group, or simply sitting quietly in a sacred space, these practices can offer comfort and support. However, if you've experienced harm in a religious context, trust yourself to set boundaries. Rebuild your faith on your terms, in a way that nurtures you, not hurts you.

Real-Life Example:

Let's take Sarah, a survivor who has always loved hiking. After everything she's been through, she struggles to trust others and feels isolated. But one day, while hiking in the woods, she feels a deep sense of peace. The quiet of the forest, the rustling of leaves in the breeze—it all feels pure, untarnished by the hurt she's experienced. There's something comforting in the natural world's ability to continue, unchanged, no matter what has happened to her. In this moment, she feels connected to something bigger than herself, a sense of peace that doesn't need words to explain it. This becomes her form of spiritual reconnection—a way to heal without the pressure of organized religion, but still with a deep sense of reverence for the world around her.

Affirmations for Spiritual Empowerment

Words have power—especially when it comes to your healing. Affirmations are statements you can say aloud or repeat to yourself that reinforce positive beliefs about who you are and what you're capable of. They help shift your mindset, moving you from a place of scarcity and fear to a mindset of abundance and hope. Spiritual affirmations can remind you that you're whole, worthy, and capable of healing—just as you are.

Here are some affirmations to help empower your spiritual journey:

- **"I am whole, just as I am."**
  This affirmation affirms your intrinsic worth, reminding you that you don't need to be fixed or changed to be valuable. You are already enough.
- **"I release what no longer serves me."**
  Sometimes, letting go of the past is the most spiritual thing you can do. This affirmation allows you to release pain, resentment, and limiting beliefs that keep you stuck.
- **"I trust myself to heal."**
  Healing is a process, and this affirmation empowers you to trust your own strength, wisdom, and resilience. You are capable of moving forward, one step at a time.

Affirmations can be used in the morning to start your day with intention, or whenever you feel overwhelmed by doubt. Over time, these words will become more than just a mantra—they'll become a part of your belief system, changing the way you see yourself and the world.

Rituals for Cleansing and Renewal

Rituals are powerful. They don't have to be religious or complex; rituals are simply actions that symbolize renewal, a fresh start, or the release of negative energy. These actions can help you mark the end of a chapter and create space for the new. Rituals are your way of saying, "I'm ready to release the past and move forward."

Here are some simple but meaningful rituals you can try:

1. Light a Candle

Candles are symbolic of light, hope, and transformation. Light a candle in a quiet moment, and as you do, visualize yourself letting go of pain, shame, or fear. Watch the flame flicker, knowing that with each flicker, you are releasing what no longer serves you. The flame represents your inner light, no matter how dim it might feel at times.

2. Write and Release

Writing is a powerful tool for processing emotions. Write down everything you want to release—fear, anger, regret, shame—then either tear the paper up or burn it (safely, of course). This ritual physically symbolizes the release of what you no longer need, offering a feeling of catharsis and closure.

3. Cleansing Bath

A cleansing bath, especially with Epsom salts or essential oils, can help you wash away negative energy. As the warm water envelops you, imagine it soothing your soul and washing away the weight of the past. You can visualize the water as a healing force that purges emotional toxins and restores peace to your body and mind.

Real-Life Example:

Let's say James, a survivor who has been carrying the weight of guilt and shame, decides to try a ritual for renewal. One evening, he lights a candle and sits quietly, focusing on the flame. As he watches the candle flicker, he allows himself to acknowledge the pain he's been holding onto, then imagines it leaving him with every breath he takes. By the time the candle burns down, he feels lighter—less weighed down by his past—and more ready to embrace the future. He repeats this ritual as often as he needs, each time feeling a little freer.

Spiritual healing doesn't have to look like anyone else's journey. It's about finding your own path to peace, your own way of reconnecting with yourself, others, or something greater. Whether you find comfort in nature, meditation, affirmations, or rituals, what matters is that you honor your own needs and take steps that feel right for you. Your healing is as unique as you are, and every small step forward is a victory. You're allowed to rebuild your faith—slowly, gently, on your own terms—and know that the journey back to trust is worth it.

Appendices

Resources for Survivors (Books, Websites, Hotlines)

Healing from sexual abuse is a deeply personal journey, but you don't have to go through it alone. Whether you're seeking books for comfort, websites for support, or hotlines for immediate help, the resources in this section are here to guide you every step of the way.

Books for Healing:

1. **"The Body Keeps the Score" by Bessel van der Kolk**
   This groundbreaking book explores how trauma reshapes both the body and the brain. Van der Kolk provides essential insights into how trauma survivors can heal, offering not just theoretical knowledge but practical advice for those living with the lasting effects of abuse.
2. **"Healing the Trauma of Abuse: A Women's Workbook" by Mary Ellen Copeland and Maxine Harris**
   This workbook offers a step-by-step approach to understanding and overcoming the trauma of abuse. Full of activities and strategies for reclaiming your life, it's especially helpful for survivors who want to dig deeper into their emotional recovery.
3. **"I Thought We Were Friends: A Story About Abuse and the Healing Process" by Ruth Fishel**
   A book that focuses on healing from emotional and sexual abuse, particularly in the context of relationships. It's written in a compassionate, easy-to-understand style that makes it accessible for people at all stages of their healing.

Trauma-Informed Therapies Explained

Healing from sexual abuse often requires specialized care. Trauma-informed therapy recognizes the complexity of the survivor's experience and offers personalized, empathetic treatment. Below are some therapeutic approaches that can support survivors in their healing journey.

1. EMDR (Eye Movement Desensitization and Reprocessing)

EMDR is a highly effective therapy for trauma survivors, particularly for those struggling with flashbacks, intrusive memories, or PTSD. This technique involves guided eye movements that help the brain process and integrate traumatic memories, reducing their emotional charge. Over time, EMDR can help you revisit painful experiences in a way that diminishes their hold on your current life, allowing for healing.

2. Cognitive Behavioral Therapy (CBT)

CBT is a structured, goal-oriented therapy that can be incredibly effective in helping survivors break the cycle of negative thoughts, self-blame, and avoidance behaviors. CBT focuses on identifying harmful patterns in thinking and replacing them with healthier ways of coping. It's an excellent choice for survivors who want practical strategies to deal with anxiety, depression, and self-esteem issues.

3. Somatic Experiencing

This therapy focuses on the connection between mind and body. It helps survivors process trauma stored in the body by focusing on physical sensations. Somatic experiencing is grounded in the idea that trauma can leave imprints in the body, which may manifest as physical symptoms. The therapist will guide you through exercises that help release these stored energies and sensations, often leading to profound emotional and physical relief.

4. Trauma-Focused Cognitive Behavioral Therapy (TF-CBT)

This approach is tailored for children, adolescents, and families. TF-CBT combines traditional CBT techniques with trauma-sensitive interventions to help young survivors process their trauma in a safe, supportive environment. The therapy is often used in conjunction with caregiver support to help the whole family heal.

5. Dialectical Behavior Therapy (DBT)

Developed to treat borderline personality disorder, DBT has been found to be highly effective for survivors of trauma. This therapy focuses on developing skills in emotional regulation, mindfulness, and interpersonal relationships. For survivors, DBT can help rebuild self-esteem, address self-harm behaviors, and strengthen emotional resilience.

6. Art Therapy

Art therapy provides survivors with a non-verbal way to express emotions that may feel too complex or overwhelming to put into words. By engaging in creative activities such as drawing, painting, or sculpting, survivors can unlock feelings and memories that may not be accessible through traditional talk therapy. Art therapy is especially helpful for those who find it hard to articulate their trauma verbally.

7. Narrative Therapy

In narrative therapy, the survivor is encouraged to rewrite the story of their life, reframing their experiences in a way that empowers them rather than defines them by the trauma. This therapy helps individuals separate themselves from their abuse, allowing them to reclaim agency and identity beyond what happened to them.

Worksheets for Emotional Processing

Processing your emotions after trauma is a powerful tool in healing. Below are some worksheets and exercises designed to guide you through the emotional healing process. Feel free to adapt them to your own needs, and consider working with a therapist to help you navigate your feelings.

1. Identifying and Challenging Negative Beliefs Worksheet

- **Instructions:** Reflect on negative beliefs or messages you may have internalized from your abuse. These could be things like, "I am not worthy of love," or "I am broken." Write down each belief and then challenge it by writing a counter-statement that reflects your true value and potential.

Example:

- Negative Belief: "I don't deserve happiness."
- Counter-Belief: "I am worthy of love, joy, and peace, and I am healing every day."

2. Safe Space Visualization Worksheet

- **Instructions:** Close your eyes and imagine a place where you feel safe, relaxed, and at peace. It could be a real place or a place you create in your mind. Draw or describe it in as much detail as possible. Use this safe space as a mental retreat whenever you need to calm your nervous system or regain a sense of control.

3. Strengths and Resilience Worksheet

- **Instructions:** Reflect on moments where you demonstrated courage, strength, or resilience during your healing process. List these moments and the specific qualities that helped you through them. Over time, this worksheet can serve as a reminder of your innate strength.

Example:

- Moment of Strength: "I reached out for help even when I was afraid."
- Resilience Trait: "Courage to ask for support and vulnerability."

4. "Who Am I Beyond My Trauma?" Worksheet

- **Instructions:** Abuse may make you feel defined by what happened, but you are so much more than your experiences. Write down the qualities, passions, and aspects of your personality that are independent of your trauma. Reconnect with your true self beyond the labels of "victim" or "survivor."

Example:

- I am someone who loves painting, has a dry sense of humor, and cares deeply for animals.
- My trauma is part of my story, but it does not define me.

5. Boundaries and Self-Care Worksheet

- **Instructions:** After trauma, it can be difficult to establish boundaries. Use this worksheet to write down your current boundaries in relationships, work, and personal life. Identify areas where you feel your boundaries are being crossed and make a plan to reassert or strengthen them. List self-care activities that nurture your emotional and physical well-being.

Example:

- Personal Boundaries: "I need time alone to recharge."
- Self-Care Activity: "Taking a walk every morning to clear my mind."

By using these resources, therapies, and worksheets, you are taking proactive steps toward healing and transformation. Remember, there is no one-size-fits-all approach to recovery, but each tool is an invitation to discover what works best for you. Healing is a journey, not a destination. Take it one day at a time, and never underestimate the power of small, consistent steps. You are worthy of a full, rich life—and you are not alone.

Author's thank you note:

To my husband the man behind everything who stood as my backbone in anything and everything without him I wouldn't have started writing in the first place. However I improved for the better everything goes for him.

Thank you,
I love you.

www.ingramcontent.com/pod-product-compliance
Lightning Source LLC
LaVergne TN
LVHW091230150826
845673LV00003B/1085

* 9 7 9 8 2 3 0 2 6 3 1 6 6 *